MAN-MADE WONDERS OF THE WORLD

Jean Cooke

First published 1980 by
Octopus Books Limited
59 Grosvenor Street
London W1

© 1980 Octopus Books Limited

ISBN 0 7064 1224 9

Produced by Mandarin Publishers Limited
22a Westlands Road
Quarry Bay, Hong Kong

Printed in Hong Kong

CONTENTS

Half-title: The Church of St Basil, in Moscow's Red Square, has eight onion-shaped domes, each differently finished and brilliantly painted.

Title page: The Great Sphinx at Giza, in Egypt, was carved from solid rock about 4,500 years ago. Its face is that of Pharaoh Khafre.

Left: King and Queen is by one of the most famous of modern sculptors, Henry Moore. He carved it in 1953, and it stands near Dumfries in Scotland.

Endpapers: Many modern man-made wonders stem from scenes like this. Masked workers in protective clothing pour molten metal into a mould during the refining process.

INTRODUCTION

The idea of compiling lists of the wonders of the world comes down to us from the ancient Greeks. The earliest known compilation was made by a Greek poet, Antipater of Sidon, just over 2,000 years ago. His 'Seven Wonders of the World', like other lists compiled by the Greeks and Romans, was almost certainly intended as a traveller's guide to the greatest sights of the world. Antipater's selection, modified by one change made in the 6th century AD, was: the Pyramids of Egypt; the Hanging Gardens of Babylon; the Temple of Artemis (Diana) at Ephesus; the Statue of Zeus at Olympia; the Mausoleum at Halicarnassus; the Colossus of Rhodes; and the Lighthouse of Alexandria (Antipater had the walls of Babylon as his seventh wonder).

The Pyramids were the oldest of these wonders of the ancient world and are also the only survivors of the seven. They were built as tombs for the pharaohs, and are almost entirely solid. The largest, the Great Pyramid of Khufu, contains about 2,300,000 huge blocks of stone and, according to the Greek historian Herodotus, 100,000 slaves laboured for 20 years to build it.

The Hanging Gardens of Babylon were the work of King Nebuchadnezzar II, a figure prominent in Old Testament lore, who reigned from 605 BC to 562 BC. Tradition has it that the gardens were built to please one of his queens who came from hilly country, and found the broad, flat plain where Babylon stood unbearable. These terrace or roof gardens, supported on arches 23 metres (75 feet) high, were planted with groves of trees and beds of flowers. The gardens were irrigated by a large reservoir, which was kept full by relays of slaves turning screw pumps to lift water up from the River Euphrates.

The Temple of Artemis was built about 550 BC by the Greeks in the city of Ephesus, which was sited on the eastern coast of Turkey. The first temple, which contained a magnificent statue of Artemis, was burned down in 356 BC by a madman named Herostratus. The temple was famous for both its size – 110 by 55 metres (350 by 180 feet) – and for its superb works of art. It was rebuilt, but this one too was destroyed, this time by the Goths, in AD 262. There was, however, to be no third temple. The original statue of Artemis had been made of gold, ebony, silver and black stone. All that now remains of the building are the foundations.

The statue of Zeus in the great temple at Olympia was said to be the masterpiece of Phidias, greatest of all Greek sculptors. Featured on coins of the period, it was covered with gold and ivory, but was destroyed in the 5th century AD.

The tomb of King Mausolus of Caria stood at Halicarnassus, a city on the Aegean coast which is now the site of the Turkish village of Bodrum. It was built in the 3rd century BC by his widow Artemesia and its magnificence has given the name 'mausoleum' to any great tomb. It was destroyed by an earthquake about 900 years ago, but some of its sculptures were saved and can be found today in the British Museum.

The Colossus of Rhodes was a statue of Helios, the sun god, which stood at the entrance to the harbour on the Greek island of Rhodes. It was about the size of a wonder of our modern world (the Statue of Liberty in New York harbour) and was made of bronze supported on a framework of stone and iron bars. Its designer, the sculptor Charles of Lindus, worked on it for 12 years, and it was completed about 280 BC. It was wrecked by an earthquake nearly 60 years later and the metal was finally sold for scrap by the Arab conquerors of Rhodes in AD 653.

Alexandria's lighthouse stood on the island of Pharos in the harbour of the Egyptian city founded by Alexander the Great. It was built about 280 BC, a multi-storied tower of white stones in whose upper windows torches and fires burned all night as a guide to shipping. This most famous of early lighthouses survived until the 14th century AD.

For centuries these seven man-made wonders were regarded as the greatest of Man's creations. Since the time of the Industrial Revolution in the mid-18th century, new materials and new techniques have enabled people to create wonders rivalling those the ancient Greeks admired. It must be remembered, however, that there were many other remarkable artefacts which existed before the time of Antipater but which were unknown to him or his fellows.

Early feats of engineering and design, such as Stonehenge in England and the hypogeum in Malta, have stirred the admiration of all ages, yet were built with simple tools and unsophisticated technology.

For every one of Antipater's wonders a modern historian could list a hundred, many in realms undreamt of by Antipater, such as electronics and space travel. Ironically our very familiarity with modern achievements often makes us overlook them and, as a result, they are denied the admiration they deserve.

Right: The ruins of the open-air theatre at Ephesus, near Seljuk, in Turkey. The theatre was completed in the reign of the Roman Emperor Trajan (AD 53–117).

HISTORIC BUILDINGS

Ever since the first Stone Age when people made themselves primitive huts with stones, sticks and mud, Man has been a builder, and every civilization bears witness to his achievements in this field. Buildings have always been the most prominent of status symbols and, for succeeding generations, a yardstick by which to measure the progress of civilization.

One indication of the way in which a superb building can express and satisfy a spiritual need is in the number of extraordinary buildings that have been connected with religion. Medieval masons laboured for many years to construct and beautify their Gothic cathedrals 'to the greater glory of God', and the same spirit informed the work of the men who built the temples of ancient Greece and Egypt, the Hindu temples of India, and the mosques of Islam.

The Egyptians were great craftsmen in stone. Their civilization depended on the River Nile, and they used it to transport huge granite blocks from the Aswan area to build their temples at Luxor, Karnak, Thebes and Memphis. These blocks were quarried by inserting wooden wedges into slots chipped in the rock. The wedges were soaked in water and the swelling wood eventually split the stone. Stones bearing the mark of this ingenious method may still be seen in abandoned quarries today.

Although they were familiar with the principle of the arch, the Egyptians, and the Greeks who followed them, preferred to use the post-and-beam method of spanning a gap. This square frame design is seen in the pillars and lintels of their stone buildings, many of which have survived. One of the extraordinary achievements of Greek temples, such as the Parthenon, is their superb proportions. The Romans, who very largely copied Greek styles, went on to make much greater use of some of their developments, such as the arch.

There are many early tombs which also testify to a religious conviction, in that they indicate a belief in life after death. Pre-eminent among tombs was the Mausoleum at Halicarnassus which unfortunately no longer exists. Its nearest rival is the superb Taj Mahal at Agra in northern India, built by Shah Jahan for the body of his favourite wife, Mumtaz-i-Mahal, in the 1600s. This breathtakingly beautiful building, a wonder of the world in any age, is now beleaguered by industrial plants and its future is threatened by the chemicals and grime of these nearby factories, as so many wonders are.

The majority of the religious wonders of the world are made of stone, and it is the skill of the masons which has given us some of our finest buildings. Perhaps the most remarkable were the great Gothic cathedrals of Europe built in the late Middle Ages. The soaring dimensions of these magnificent buildings were partly inspired, it is said, by the towering avenues of trees and the natural arcades formed by their branches which so deeply impressed the masons.

The need for adequate defences has also created some wonderful achievements of construction. The main buildings used for defence were castles, and several of those which survive are truly remarkable. Among the most outstanding are the Alcazár at Segovia in Spain and Windsor Castle in England, both being the homes of kings as well as strongholds. Neuschwanstein Castle in Bavaria is a modern imitation, but nonetheless quite remarkable. Built in the late 19th century on the orders of King Ludwig II of Bavaria, who was mentally unstable, it glorified his love of the extravagant and the romantic, particularly the music of the composer Richard Wagner. It is, as it was intended to be, the last word in fairy-tale castles.

As the desire for luxury and beauty supplanted the need for security and efficiency, the castle gave way to the palace. Outstanding among such buildings is the famous palace of Versailles, built by King Louis XIV of France in the 17th century. It is remarkable for its size and for the lavish ornaments and furnishings in many of its hundreds of rooms.

In the 19th and 20th centuries the emphasis has been on developing and using new materials and methods of construction. The real innovation of this period is the skyscraper, originally designed to make the maximum use of restricted and expensive sites. The tallest skyscraper in the world is the 110-storey Sears Tower in Chicago, completed in 1973. It overtook the World Trade Centre in New York City, which had held the record for only a year. The most famous of all skyscrapers is the Empire State Building, also in New York, which at 449 metres (1,472 feet) held the record as the world's tallest building for 41 years. However, all these giant skyscrapers are dwarfed by two other structures: the CN Tower in Toronto, the tallest self-supporting tower at 555.3 metres (1,822 feet), and the Warszawa Radio Mast in Poland, which reaches 646 metres (2,120 feet) into the sky.

Previous pages: **Hagia Sophia, in Istanbul, built as a Christian church in AD 532–537, is now a museum. The Turks added the minarets in the 15th century.**

Right: **Reflections in the glass walls of a skyscraper in Houston, Texas. This is an example of the adventurous use of modern materials and methods in 20th century urban architecture.**

The Parthenon stands on the Acropolis, or 'upper city', overlooking ancient Athens. It was a temple to Athena Parthenos, the 'virgin Athena', who was the city's patron goddess, and it was built in 447–432 BC. The architects were Ictinus and Callicrates, and Phidias, the finest of Greek sculptors, decorated it with carvings and statues.

Delphi was thought by the ancient Greeks to be the centre of the world. It had a world famous oracle which was consulted by statesmen and private citizens alike. The ruins were excavated from 1892 onwards. This stunning building was the *tholos*, possibly an administrative centre.

Mont St Michel is a fortified abbey, standing on a steep rocky island off the coast of Normandy. A causeway connects it to the mainland. The abbey was founded in 966, and some of the buildings date from that period. Construction went on until the 1400s, when the ramparts were finished. The most notable of its buildings is La Merveille (1203–1228), containing cloisters and halls.

The Taj Mahal, at Agra in India, was built by the Mughal emperor Shah Jahan as a tomb for his favourite wife, Mumtaz-i-Mahal. It is considered by many to be one of the most beautiful buildings in the world.

Machu Picchu, the 'Lost City of the Incas', lay hidden in the jungle for 300 years until the American explorer Hiram Bingham discovered it in 1911. Its buildings include temples constructed with blocks of hand-carved granite, some weighing more than 10 tonnes. The last surviving Inca warriors retreated to this mountain stronghold after the Spanish conquest in the 1530s.

Neuschwanstein Castle in Bavaria was built in the late 1800s for Bavaria's eccentric king, Ludwig II. Ludwig's instructions for the design were greatly influenced by the German Romantic movement. The castles' majestic rooms were decorated as if they were settings for the 'Ring' cycle of operas, written by Richard Wagner.

A floodlit view of the Château de Chenonceaux, which stands on the River Cher not far from Tours in the Loire Valley of France. It was built between 1515 and 1523, and for many years was the home of Diane de Poitiers, mistress of Henri II. The original château was the rectangular block on the right, which stands on piles in the river. The bridge was built across the river between 1556 and 1559, and the gallery over it twenty years later.

The Leaning Tower of Pisa was built between 1174 and 1350 as a bell-tower for the cathedral beside it. The tower began to lean because of subsidence even while it was being built, and it is now 4.2 metres (14 feet 10 inches) out of line.

The twin towers of the World Trade Centre in New York City reflect the setting sun across the Hudson River. It is New York's tallest building, and at 411 metres (1,350 feet) the second highest skyscraper in the world. The two 110-storey towers dominate the city's financial district, and are owned by the Port Authority of New York and New Jersey. The building was opened in 1973, and was plagued by fires for the first two years of its existence. The New York State Government occupies 55 floors in one of the towers.

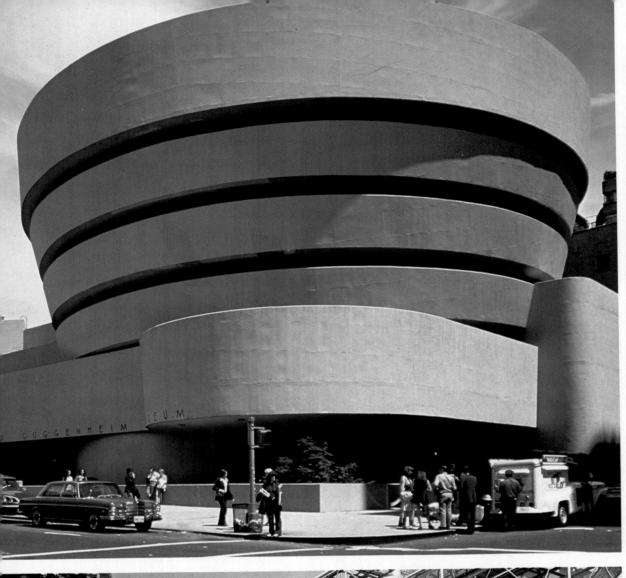

Left: The Guggenheim Museum of Non-Objective Art in New York City has an extremely unusual design. Inside, paintings are hung along the walls of a spiral concrete ramp which winds its way up to a glazed domed roof. The museum was designed by one of the greatest American architects, Frank Lloyd Wright (1869–1959) and was completed and opened the year after his death.

Right: A series of sail-like overlapping shells forms the roof of the Sydney Opera House, one of the most remarkable buildings of the 20th century. It was designed by the Danish architect Joern Utzon. The work began in 1959, and was completed in 1973, at a cost of five times the original estimate, more than $100 million Australian dollars.

Left: The Georges Pompidou National Centre for Art and Culture in Paris was opened in 1977 to the accompaniment of a storm of praise and criticism. A network of pipes supports this amazing building, which is constructed of concrete and glass.

ROADS, BRIDGES AND CANALS

Recent advances in overland transport have been so marked that it is easy to overlook the achievements of earlier engineers. Modern highways and bridges are, admittedly, masterpieces of engineering and employ some remarkable materials and techniques, but it must not be forgotten that the Romans left a network of highways which by AD 200 totalled about 80,000 kilometres (50,000 miles). These were solid, well-made roads, on a deep foundation of stones covered with concrete and topped with hard stone sets. Minor roads extended over a distance about four times as long. Portions of original Roman road can still be seen, for example, along the Via Appia, which runs south-east from Rome.

After the Romans, the art of road building fell into decline but revived slowly from the 18th century onwards. An early pioneer of this revival was the remarkable Englishman John Metcalf. Although he lost his sight as a boy, his disability did not prevent him from making great advances in the art of road building. Modern highways, however, really owe their existence to a Scot, John Loudon McAdam, who invented the macadamized surface of rolled, crushed stones.

The first of the truly modern express highway networks were the *Autobahnen*, built in Germany in the 1930s by the Nazis for military purposes. Since the end of World War II in 1945 and the proliferation of the car, major highway networks have been constructed in all parts of the world. One of the most extraordinary is the Pan American Highway, a road system extending from the United States south to Chile. An ambitious aspect of its construction is the section through the Darien Gap, a stretch of dense jungle in Panama.

Jungle is not the only obstacle to highways. The most frequently encountered is water, and from ancient times people have devoted much energy and skill to building bridges. Again, the Romans were the earliest of the great bridge builders, though few of their bridges now survive. One of the most remarkable of bridges was the old London Bridge. It was begun in 1176, and lasted until 1831. Its 19 arches stood on huge piers that effectively blocked half the width of the River Thames.

Timber, brick and stone were the only materials available to bridge builders until the late 1700s, when large iron castings became generally available. The world's first all cast-iron bridge was built in England over the River Severn at Coalbrookdale in 1779, and is still standing. For

the next century or so the largest bridges, and those with the longest spans, were of the suspension type, with cables made of iron or steel links, or high-tensile steel wires. The development of steel manufacture in the late 1800s led to the construction of many steel bridges. The high-level bridge over the River Tay in Scotland was one of the longest, but in 1879, a year after it opened, 13 of its main spans were blown down in a gale, taking with them a trainload of people. This disaster prompted extensive research into the effects of wind on bridges, the first result of which was the rail bridge over the River Forth. Opened in 1890, and designed to cope with extreme wind pressures, it was built on the cantilever principle, with great arches extending from three tall steel piers, and no supporting structure underneath. The bridge, still in use, remains an outstanding example of construction and design.

The world's longest bridge is the Lake Pontchartrain Causeway in Louisiana, with a total length of 47 kilometres (29 miles). This bridge is mostly made of pre-stressed concrete spans. Another extra-long structure is the Chesapeake Bay Bridge-Tunnel, nearly 29 kilometres (18 miles) long.

Inland waterways as transport routes are still of major importance; rivers of Europe, the Soviet Union and the United States are linked by huge networks of canals. A remarkable example is the St Lawrence Seaway, which links the St Lawrence River and the Atlantic Ocean with the Great Lakes. Between Lake Superior, the largest and furthest inland of the Great Lakes, and the Atlantic, the water level rises 180 metres (600 feet). The seaway, which is 293 kilometres (182 miles) long, accounts for almost one third of this rise. Canals and locks linking lakes Superior and Huron, and Erie and Ontario, account for most of the rest of the rise.

The construction of the Suez Canal was relatively simple, since the Mediterranean and Red seas are at about the same level, and the land between them is comparatively flat. The world's other great waterway, the Panama Canal, constructed by American engineers and opened in 1914, presented much greater engineering problems. The Isthmus of Panama, through which it runs, is a mass of hills, swamps and impenetrable, fever-ridden jungle, and the Atlantic and Pacific oceans which it connects are at different levels. Its construction was made possible by one of the greatest engineering inventions, the lock, by which waterways at different levels may be linked without a great uncontrolled flow of water from the higher to the lower level. The first canal to have locks was the Bereguardo Canal, near Milan, which was completed in 1458.

Right: Fast-moving traffic draws vivid lines of light in this picture of a neon-lit intersection in the Ginza district of Tokyo. Ginza is a lively area, noted for its shops and nightclubs, and, like other parts of Tokyo, for its traffic jams.

Below: The Europa Bridge, carrying the Brenner Autobahn which links Innsbruck with the Brenner Pass and Italy. It is a fine example of modern bridge construction in prestressed concrete. Such bridges, which often have long, slender spans, use much less material than conventional structures built with reinforced concrete.

The Pont du Gard aqueduct near Nîmes in southern France carried water across the valley of the River Gard to the Roman city of Nemausus. It was built about AD 14, and is perfectly preserved. It is 269 metres (882 feet) long and 47 metres (155 feet) high above the river, and is one of the finest examples of Roman bridge-building. *Inset:* An even older bridge – the 4,000-year-old clapper bridge over the River Dart at Postbridge in Devon. A clapper bridge consists of large flat slabs of stone supported on rough stone piers.

Left: Ironbridge, near Coalbrookdale in Salop, was the world's first large-scale cast-iron bridge, and it is still open to pedestrians. It was built in 1779 by the ironmaster Abraham Darby so that his workpeople and wagons could cross the River Severn. It has a span of 30 metres (100 feet), and its main ribs, 21 metres (70 feet) long, were each cast in one piece and fastened together by wedges, without bolts or rivets.

Above: The Golden Gate Bridge crosses the Golden Gate, the channel at the entrance to San Francisco Bay, and is one of the world's most eye catching bridges. The span between the twin towers is 1,280 metres (4,200 feet) long. The bridge carries a six-lane road, part of US Highway 101, and footpaths. The two steel cables supporting the deck are 930 millimetres ($36\frac{1}{2}$ inches) in diameter. The roadway is 67 metres (220 feet) above the water, and ships pass under it all day to and from the busy harbour. The bridge was completed in 1937.

Below: Water crosses water: an aqueduct carries the Mittelland Canal over the River Weser at Minden, in northern West Germany. It is one of the canal's greatest engineering works.
The canal links the Dortmund–Ems Canal with the River Elbe.

Right: The Corinth Canal runs for 6.3 kilometres (4 miles) through the Isthmus of Corinth, which links the Peloponnese Peninsula with the Greek mainland. It was cut through the solid rock of the isthmus between 1882 and 1893. The channel is only 25 metres (80 feet) wide.

WALSRODE

Left: The Rialto Bridge over the Grand Canal in Venice. The Grand Canal is the largest of the 150 canals that serve as the city's streets, and these canals are crossed by about 300 bridges. The Grand Canal is S-shaped, and about 3.2 kilometres (2 miles) long. The Rialto Bridge was built in its present form between 1588 and 1592. The bridge is lined on either side with narrow shops, though these were not part of the original design by Antonio da Ponte. He built it with open arches, and shaped it so that an armed galley could pass under it.

Above: Amsterdam in The Netherlands is another city of canals, often called 'the Venice of the North'. There are 80 kilometres of canals, spanned by 300 bridges and flanked by narrow roadways, which divide the city into about 70 islands. Amsterdam was founded in the Middle Ages when the River Amstel was dammed to form a harbour – hence the city's name. This view, down one of the oldest canals, shows the *Schreyerstoren* or 'Weepers' Tower', which was part of the medieval fortifications of the city.

TRANSPORT

Although the history of transport begins with the invention of the wheel, the greatest advances have been made in the past 200 years or so. Until the beginning of the 19th century people travelled as they had done for thousands of years – on foot, on horseback, in vehicles drawn by animals, and by water. Boats were driven by the wind and/or by men pulling at oars. The revolution in forms of transport began in 1769 when the French engineer Nicolas Cugnot built a steam carriage for hauling guns. Although it had to stop every quarter of an hour to build up steam, its hesitant passage marked the beginning of a new era.

From then on road transport progressed less surely than other forms. Steam carriages ran for a while, but were greatly hampered by the poor roads of the time. The next real development came in 1885 and 1886, when the Germans Karl Benz and Gottlieb Daimler built the first practical motor cars powered by internal combustion engines. Since that time cars of all kinds have proliferated, and this expansion is one of the wonders of the 20th century. Indeed, if one car had to represent all that the 20th century has to offer in the way of improving transport technology and greater comfort, the Rolls-Royce Silver Ghost might be a fitting early example.

The Moon buggies which went with the last three Apollo space missions are remarkable cars, designed for a purpose which the ancient Greeks could scarcely have imagined, and are electrically powered with a top speed of 18 kph (11 mph).

Self-powered trains came a little after Cugnot's pioneer road vehicle, although wooden railroads with horse-drawn trucks or man-handled cars had been in use in the coalmines since the 1500s. The world's first locomotive was built in 1804 by the Cornish engineer Richard Trevithick, but the first true wonder of rail transport was George Stephenson's locomotive *Rocket* which won the Rainhill Trials near Liverpool in 1829. This pioneering example of the efficient use of steam power on the railways still stands in the Science Museum in London, a lasting testament to engineering skill. One of the most powerful locomotives ever built was the 'Big Boy', owned by the Union Pacific Railroad in the United States. Completed in 1941, it had a capacity of 6,000 horsepower (4.48 megawatts). In the late 1970s the Japanese built experimental models of an even more wonderful train, the Maglev, which is held clear of the track and propelled at great speed by magnetic force.

Size and speed have been important criteria for assessing the wonders of sea transport, ever since Isambard Kingdom Brunel built the *Great Britain*. This ship, launched in 1843, was at that time the largest iron ship built. After 41 years of active service it spent a further half-century as a storage hulk in the Falkland Islands, before being scuttled in shallow water. In 1970 she was refloated and towed back to a permanent berth in the Bristol dock where she was built.

The largest and perhaps the most luxurious passenger ship ever built was the *Queen Elizabeth*, which made her maiden voyage in 1940. Unfortunately, after she had been withdrawn from service, she was destroyed by fire in 1972. Even the *Queen Elizabeth* was small compared with today's supertankers, which are more than 370 metres (1,200 feet) long, and can carry 450,000 tonnes of petroleum. A remarkable feature of these huge ships is that they can be handled by very small crews, often numbering less than 30, unlike the giant liners of the first half of the 20th century which had crews hundreds strong, as well as a full hotel staff,

One of the most remarkable vessels of today is the hovercraft, invented by Christopher Cockerell in 1955. These air-cushion vehicles, as they are also known, float above rather than on the surface of the sea, so reducing drag and enabling them to attain greater speeds than conventional craft. However, because they float on an air cushion, there is some doubt as to whether hovercraft are strictly ships or aircraft.

Flight has always been the most fascinating and elusive of all modes of transport, and it was not until 1903 that Orville Wright's *Flyer I* made the first powered flight of a heavier-than-air craft. Almost all the basic principles of modern aircraft are incorporated in this small, flimsy craft which is preserved in the National Air and Space Museum in Washington DC. The Wright brothers' first flight lasted 12 seconds and covered 37 metres (120 feet), yet this short journey was just as wonderful as the transatlantic flights of the supersonic *Concorde* aircraft in the 1970s and 1980s.
For sheer versatility, the helicopter is perhaps the most remarkable of aircraft. Able to hover and fly forwards and backwards, it is without parallel as a rescue vehicle and airborne workhorse. The enormous size and beauty of the *Graf Zeppelin* airship also deserves mention. This most famous of lighter-than-air vehicles operated a regular commercial service between Europe and South America for four years in the 1930s.

Previous pages: **The 'Bullet' train on Japan's New Tokaido Railway averages 166.2kph (103.3mph) on its regular run between Osaka and Tokyo.**

Right: **A superb diesel-electric locomotive at the head of a freight train at Miami, on the Florida and East Coast Railroad in the United States.**

A pair of traction engines, the steam locomotives of the roads. Traction engines were first built in the early 1800s, and they remained in use for drawing heavy loads until the 1920s. They were made with grooved wheels to grip greasy roads.

A replica of the *Rocket*, the railway locomotive built by the British engineer George Stephenson. The original engine, which is preserved in London's Science Museum, won the Rainhill Trials at Liverpool in 1829 and set new standards of reliability.

Above: A 1925 van version of the Ford 'Model T'. This vehicle was in production from 1908 to 1927, and altogether 15,007, 033 Model Ts were built. *Below:* In contrast, a sleek streamlined Porsche of the 1970s. The Porsche 930 Turbo has an extremely powerful engine.

Right: Formula 1 cars racing on a circuit in Austria. These specially-built cars have engines of up to 12 cylinders, with a limit of 3,000c.c. unsupercharged or 1,500 supercharged. The cars are single-seater. All now have the engine behind the driver.

Above: A hovercraft speeding across Sydney Harbour. The hovercraft represents one of the greatest revolutions in boat design for centuries: it was the idea of a British electronics engineer, Sir Christopher Cockerell, who designed it in 1955.

Left: The giant oil tanker *Esso Cambria*, 249,952 tonnes, was launched in 1969 at the Verolme shipyard at Rotterdam. It is 348 metres (1,141 feet) long. Supertankers of this kind carry very small crews, sometimes numbering only 30 men.

A Whirlwind helicopter delivers stores to the Royal Naval ice patrol ship, *H.M.S. Endurance.* The first successful helicopters were built in the 1930s: they have since been adapted to serve many uses acting as, for example, flying cranes, rescue vehicles, short-haul carriers, and even as aids to traffic control.

The Anglo-French *Concorde* was the first supersonic airliner to go into regular service. The 2,170kph (1,350mph) jet began transatlantic flights in May 1976, reducing journey times to a little over three hours – and in December 1979 a Concorde flew the Atlantic in just under three hours. In terms of design and construction these aircraft were the most expensive ever built, and only 16 were completed.

The Curtiss-Wright 16K is a typical example of a small aircraft, built in the period between the two world wars – a biplane with a single engine and two open cockpits. The fighter aircraft of World War I were constructed along similar lines.

The Boeing 747 was the first jumbo-jet. It first flew in 1969 and went into regular service in 1970. It can carry nearly 500 passengers in its long, wide body, and has proved the most popular and reliable jet airliner of modern times.

The Brazilian aircraft carrier *Minas Gerais* anchored in harbour. The first ship of this kind, providing a mobile base for aircraft, went into service with the U.S. Navy in 1922, and in World War II, there were more than 150 in service.

The F-14 two-seater multi-rôle fighter plane, which went into service in the early 1970s, was designed for use aboard aircraft carriers. It has a maximum speed of more than 2,500kph (1,550mph), and its wings have a variable sweep.

Harrier fighter planes swoop over the Arctic. The plane
is the western world's only fixed-wing V/STOL
(Vertical/short take-off and landing) strike fighter.
The prototype of this remarkable aircraft flew
in 1966. The Harrier's speed at low level
is more than 1,186kph (737mph), and
when diving it can travel at 1.3
times the speed of sound.
From vertical take-off
to a height of 12,200
metres (40,000 feet)
takes a mere 2 minutes
22.7 seconds.

GREAT ENGINEERING FEATS

The most remarkable feats of engineering are often embodied in great buildings although the distinction between building and engineering is often very hard to draw. The Great Pyramid, for example, is in a limited sense a building (though no one lived or worked in or actively used its interior) and it is really a great piece of engineering, constructed as it was with a minimum of mechanical help. It is thought that gangs of slaves built a spiral ramp of earth and rubble around the growing pyramid, and then hauled the huge blocks of stone on rollers up the ramp to the required place.

England's finest prehistoric stone circle is Stonehenge. Begun about the same time as the pyramids, it took final shape 1,400 years later. The double ring of blue stones which at one time stood in the centre came from Wales, 390km (240 miles) away. Some of the huge blocks of sandstone which form part of this famous stone circle weighed about the same as the blocks of which the pyramids are made.

Silbury Hill, not far from Stonehenge and constructed about the same time for a purpose as yet undiscovered, is the largest artificial hill in Europe. It contains about 340,000 cubic metres (12,000,000 cubic feet) of soil.

Perhaps one of the most remarkable structures is the Great Wall of China, the longest single man-made object in the world. The Romans were also skilled wall builders, and the best preserved of their defence works is Hadrian's Wall, built about 120 AD to defend the northern limits of the Roman Empire in Britain.

Three of the world's most extraordinary temples were made, not by building, but by cutting into rock. The most primitive is the Hypogeum in Malta, a series of chambers hollowed out of the rock one under the other. The rock temples of Abu Simbel in Egypt were cut into the rocky wall of the River Nile by order of Pharaoh Rameses II in the 11th century BC. The site now lies under the waters of Lake Nasser, although the temple had been re-erected on nearby high ground in the 1960s. The most modern of the rock-cut temples is at Kailasanatha, Ellora, India, constructed in the 8th–10th centuries AD. It is perhaps the most elaborate of India's many rock-cut temples, the earliest of which were based on existing caves. The Ellora temple is very large and the halls, shrines and pillars which are carved from the solid rock are profusely decorated with carvings.

Many people tend to think of engineering in terms of metalwork. A remarkable early example of the craft is the Iron Pillar at Delhi, made by Hindu craftsmen in the 4th century AD. It stands 7 metres (23 feet) high and has never rusted, even after centuries of exposure to weathering. In more modern times, the most familiar example of engineering in iron and steel is the Eiffel Tower, built in 1889, though similar methods have been used for many kinds of structures, such as bridges.

A great advance in construction techniques became possible with the modern development of concrete. Concrete was first used in the second Temple of Concord, erected in Rome in 121 BC, but its modern form, reinforced concrete, was largely invented by two Frenchmen, Joseph Monier and Francois Hennebique, mid-way through the 19th century. This combination of moulded concrete with steel rods for strength has led to some dazzling dramatic constructions, such as the Palazzetto della Sport erected in Rome for the 1960 Olympic Games. It was designed by Pier Luigi Nervi and Annibale Vitellozzi, and has a shallow shell dome 60 metres (200 feet) in diameter. It was erected in just 40 days from prefabricated parts.

In 1927 a French engineer, Eugene Freyssinet, perfected pre-stressed concrete, in which the reinforcement is made of high-tensile steel wires which are put under tension before the concrete mix is cast around them. In this way a concrete beam can be produced that is under compression longitudinally, so giving it a much greater load-bearing strength than conventional reinforced concrete. As a result it is possible to use much more slender members to cross great distances. Many modern constructions owe their form and apparent lightness to pre-stressed concrete, for example the 45-metres (150-feet) straight span of the British Airways hangars at London Airport.

A very different kind of engineering is required for another of today's man-made wonders, undersea exploration. Two important aspects of underwater exploration are the vehicles used for taking scientists down to the sea bed and the undersea habitats where people can live and work for weeks at a time. The vehicle used for the deepest dive ever, into the Mariana Trench in the Pacific Ocean, was the bathyscaphe, a steel sphere suspended from a large float filled with petrol. The petrol is lighter than water and keeps the craft afloat; when water is admitted into the tank the petrol is compressed and loses buoyancy, and the bathyscaphe sinks. Ascent is accomplished by jettisoning metal ballast.

Previous page: **Stonehenge, the great prehistoric monument on Salisbury Plain, was begun about 2700 BC. Its original purpose is still not known.**

Right: **Al Khasnah, in the ruined city of Petra in Jordan, is the finest of some 750 tombs which were cut out of solid rock. It dates from about AD 120.**

The rock-dwellings at Uçhisar, in central Turkey, have been carved out of earth pillars. The pillars originally had caps of lava but these were removed, partly for safety and partly to provide building stone. The houses are still in use, and many now have electricity. The pillars were formed out of tuff, a rock made of ash and dust from the nearby volcano, Mount Ercyias.

Right: The Pyramids of Giza are the sole survivors of the original Seven Wonders of the World. They were built as tombs by the pharaohs Khufu, Khafre and Menkaure about 2600–2500 BC. Most of their outer casing of white stone has been removed.

Below: The Great Wall of China, which was the largest engineering feat ever undertaken. It runs for more than 2,410 kilometres (1,500 miles) and stands about 8 metres (26 feet) high. It took nearly two thousand years to construct, and was finished around 1600 AD.

Above: A giant pipe snakes its way across the Great Canadian Oil Sands plant near McMurray, in Alberta. This is the biggest mining operation in Canada, and has been set up to extract petroleum from the bituminous sand deposits in the valley of the Athabasca River. They are the world's largest deposits of bituminous sands, and contain about 13 per cent of tarry substances, from which oil and gas can be recovered.

Left: Opening up a new tunnel 43 metres (140 feet) below ground in a diamond mine near Pretoria, South Africa. The miners use air-powered and water-cooled drills to cut their way through the rock, known as kimberlite or blue ground, which forms 'pipes' in which the diamonds are found. Many diamond mines are very deep, the deepest being 3.84 kilometres (2.38 miles) below ground, at Carltonville, South Africa.

The Eiffel Tower was built for the Paris Exposition of 1889, and has remained as a landmark in the city ever since. It is a latticework of wrought iron 300 metres (984 feet) tall, and was the world's highest structure for many years. It is topped by a television mast, and contains restaurants and a weather station. The designer was the French engineer Alexandre Gustave Eiffel, who also built the interior framework of the Statue of Liberty in New York Harbour.

Left: The Atomium, which was built for the World Fair held at Brussels in 1958. A theme of the exposition was atomic physics. This piece of engineering represented the atomic structure of a molecule – to a scale of about 200,000 million times as large as in nature. Stairways and lifts linked the spheres representing the atoms. The lower spheres contain the exhibits, and the top sphere is a restaurant.

Below: An offshore drilling platform used for tapping petroleum and natural gas beneath the sea bed. These giants of modern technology are constructed at shipyards and towed to their working site, where underwater legs are lowered to rest on the sea bottom. A typical offshore platform has, in addition to the drilling machinery and its supporting derrick, well-equipped rooms for the crew to eat, sleep and enjoy recreation time in. A platform allows helicopters to land and take off.

CENTRE NATIONAL DE LA RECHERCHE SCIENTIFIQUE

INVENTIONS AND DISCOVERIES

The story of civilization over the centuries is really the story of Man's ability to invent, for each new contrivance marked a step forward towards the sophisticated technological society we have today. The list of inventions is endless, and many, such as textiles, metal-working and irrigation, stem from prehistoric times. However, many of the greatest contributions to progress are conceptual, such as language and speech, democracy or the development of ideologies. The advance of human knowledge has been hastened by the development of writing, which has enabled each generation to pass on its accumulated wisdom to the next. Animals are capable of passing on inherited skills – some of these skills, such as the air-conditioned nest construction of the termites, are highly complex – but their capabilities are limited when compared with Man's enormous capacity to acquire and communicate knowledge.

From writing came one of the wonders of the modern world, the invention of printing. Some form of printing has been practised for a very long time, but printing from movable type which can be used repeatedly was first tried by a goldsmith from Mainz in Germany, Johannes Gutenberg, halfway through the 15th century.

In the field of optics, two inventions at opposite ends of the scale have helped to change Man's ideas about his world. They are the microscope, which opened people's eyes to things too small for them to see, and the telescope, which over the centuries has shown us the immensity of the universe beyond our Earth. Both were the products of Dutch genius: the microscope was the work of Anton van Leeuwenhoek, a draper and amateur scientist, while the telescope is attributed to Hans Lippershey, a spectacle maker. Both inventions were made in the early 1600s, though some people believe that another Dutchman, Zacharias Janssen, was the inventor of both, a decade earlier.

Amid so many inventions, each of them having far-reaching effects on Man's development and history, it is difficult to indentify the most wonderful. However, there have been a number which, like printing, have set mankind off along a new and exciting path. These include innovations which vary from the first musical instruments to the silicon chip and to the development of atomic power.

The first full-scale nuclear power plant went into operation at Calder Hall in northern England in 1956, and today nuclear power plants are in operation in many parts of the world. Their use however, could result in an accident which would have terrible and far-reaching consequences. Work is currently going on to harness the power of the atom in the same way that the Sun produces its energy – by the fusion of atoms rather than by splitting them, the method now used in atomic power stations. The technical problems are enormous, but the prospects are good because the fuel used in such a process is heavy hydrogen, an isotope of hydrogen, readily extracted from water.

The earliest electronic devices were the valves or vacuum tubes which formed the heart of all radio and television sets until the 1960s. They were invented in the early 1900s. A valve is bulky and requires heat in order to work, and the signals in it flow through a vacuum. More recently, research has concentrated on solid substances, known as semiconductors. Semiconductors are neither good insulators nor good conductors of current. There are a number of these substances, but the two most often used are silicon and germanium. By adding carefully regulated quantities of other elements scientists can convert semiconductors into substances that can conduct currents in a controlled way. This is the basis of the transistor, the tiny solid-state device which has now almost completely replaced the valve.

While the physicists have been putting electrical currents to work for us in more and more ways, the chemists have turned their attention to creating new raw materials to supplement or replace those available in nature. These materials go under the general name of plastics – that is, they can be moulded. Chemists make plastics from synthetic resins, using chemicals extracted from such natural materials as coal, limestone and petroleum. The first successful plastics material was Celluloid, made in 1869, and the first man-made fibre which could be used for clothes was rayon, produced in 1884.

Another wonder of the modern world is the laser, a device which amplifies light, and concentrates its beam so that it does not spread out as much as the light from an ordinary light source, for example a car's headlamp. Laser beams can be used to carry electric signals over long distances with very little interference. Concentrated through a lens they produce intense heat, which can be used to cut metal, or for delicate surgical operations, such as welding a detached retina back into place in a person's eye.

Previous pages: **A solar furnace at Font-Romeu, in the Pyrennees Mountains of France. Mirrors on the hillside direct the sun's rays on to the huge convex mirror, which focuses them on the furnace building in front.**

Right: **The microscope made and used by the versatile English scientist Robert Hooke, in about 1665. The main body, which contains the main lens, is made of cardboard covered with red, gold-stamped leather.**

Above: The astronomical clock at Hampton Court Palace, near London, was made for Henry VIII in 1540 by Nicholas Oursian. It shows the hour, the month, the day of the month, the number of days since the beginning of the year, the phases of the Moon, and it also indicates high water at London Bridge.

Right: A modern reconstruction of the spinning jenny, patented by James Hargraves in 1770. This machine, which spun thread on 16 spindles at once, was one of the pioneering inventions which spurred on the Industrial Revolution in Britain.

The bell telegraph receiver, invented by Sir Charles Tilston Bright in 1876. Bright was a pioneer of long-distance telegraphy, laying the first cable under the Atlantic between Ireland and Newfoundland, and also the first cable between Britain and India, by way of the Mediterranean Sea. This receiver was just one of a number of his inventions in the field of communications.

Johannes Gutenberg's invention in the 1440s of a printing press which used movable type was a great development in the field of communications. The first advance on this wooden press came in 1798 with the third Earl Stanhope's invention of the iron press. The press shown here was made in 1837. Though all metal, it retained most of the features of the press of 1440.

Above: The *Kräuterbuch* (Book of Herbs) was produced by the German botanist Adam Lonitzer in 1557. It is typical of the books produced in the early years of printing.

Right: Taking a proof of the front page of a London daily newspaper. Most of the type is set by machine, though the basic process is one that Gutenberg would have recognized. Once the news pages have been set the paper is printed and delivered within a period of about 12 hours.

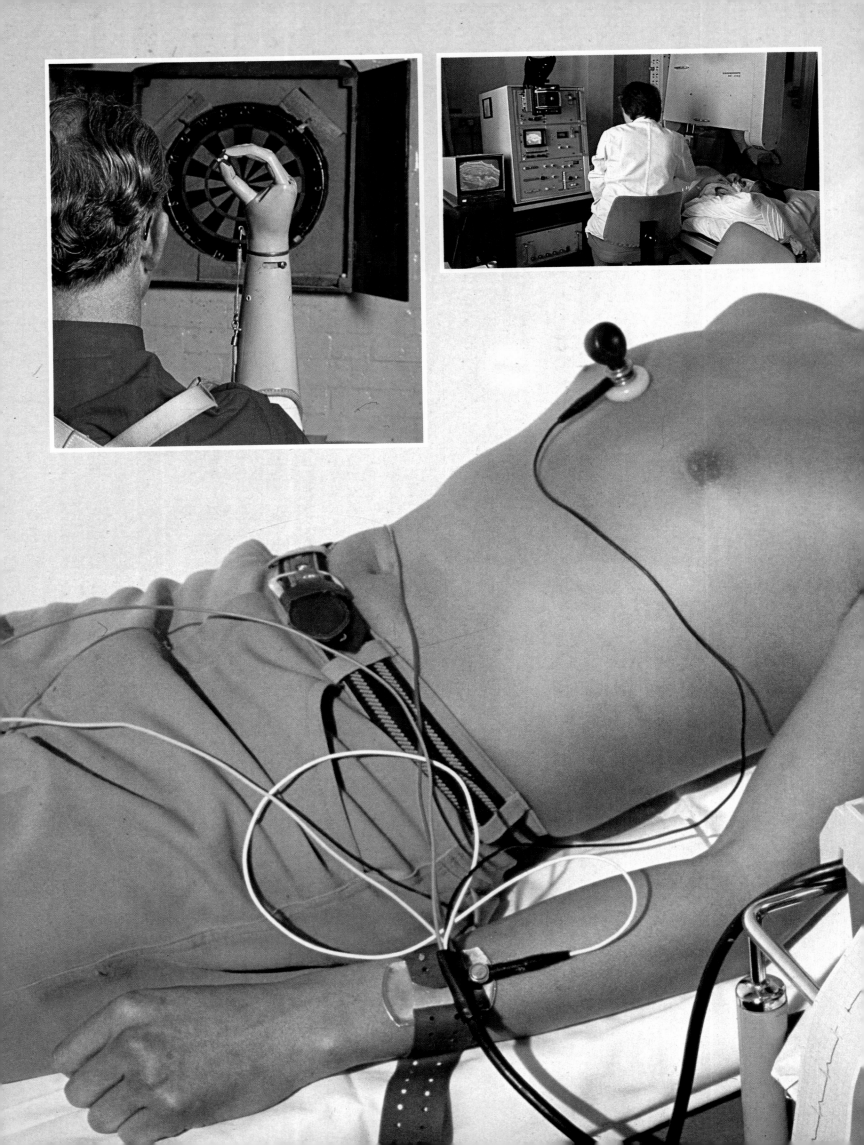

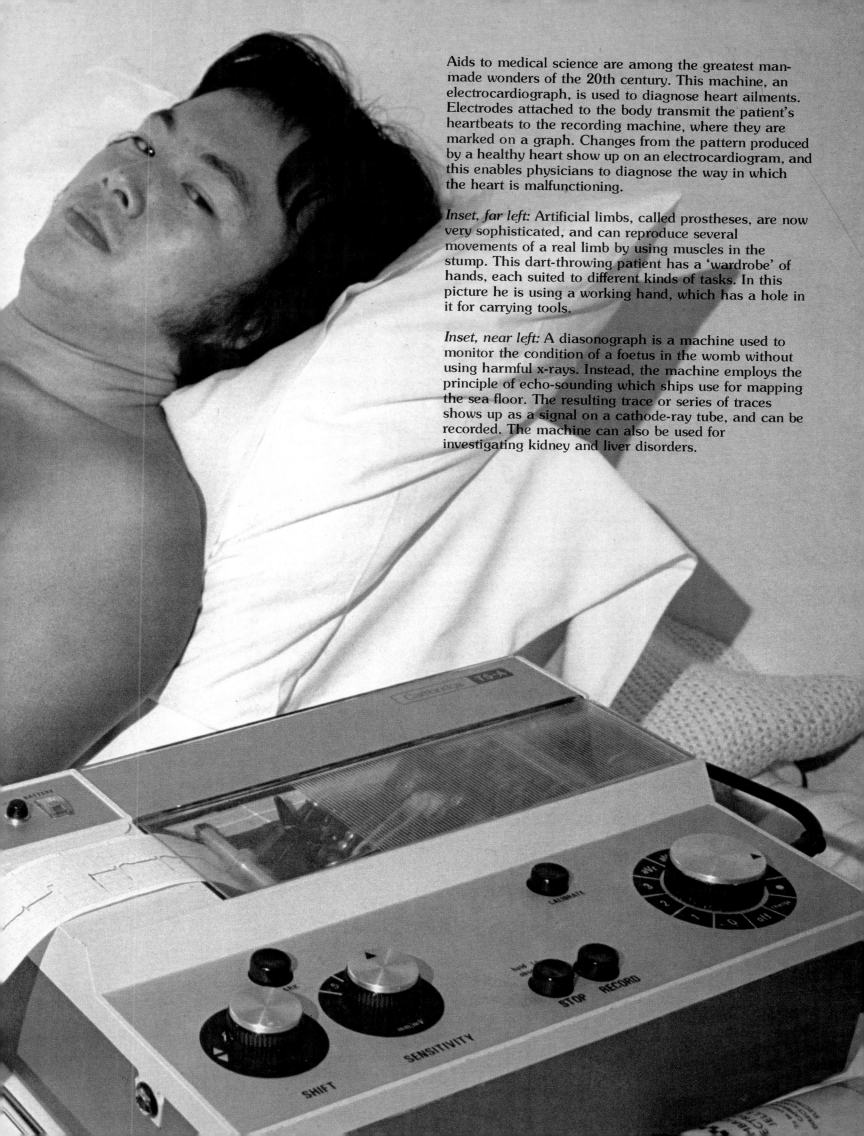

Aids to medical science are among the greatest man-made wonders of the 20th century. This machine, an electrocardiograph, is used to diagnose heart ailments. Electrodes attached to the body transmit the patient's heartbeats to the recording machine, where they are marked on a graph. Changes from the pattern produced by a healthy heart show up on an electrocardiogram, and this enables physicians to diagnose the way in which the heart is malfunctioning.

Inset, far left: Artificial limbs, called prostheses, are now very sophisticated, and can reproduce several movements of a real limb by using muscles in the stump. This dart-throwing patient has a 'wardrobe' of hands, each suited to different kinds of tasks. In this picture he is using a working hand, which has a hole in it for carrying tools.

Inset, near left: A diasonograph is a machine used to monitor the condition of a foetus in the womb without using harmful x-rays. Instead, the machine employs the principle of echo-sounding which ships use for mapping the sea floor. The resulting trace or series of traces shows up as a signal on a cathode-ray tube, and can be recorded. The machine can also be used for investigating kidney and liver disorders.

Left: The silicon chip is the heart of calculators and many forms of electronic devices. This magnified picture – the original is only about 3 millimetres square – shows the mass of transistors and circuits.

Right: Nuclear energy is widely regarded as the main power source of the future. This is part of the fast reactor at Dounreay in Scotland, part of the United Kingdom's atomic energy system. Heat from the reactor is used to produce steam, which in turn drives turbo-generators to produce electricity.

Below: A close-up of a laser. A laser beam is a concentrated, narrow shaft of light which does not spread and become diffuse in the way that ordinary light does. Laser beams can be used to cut holes in metal, drill diamonds, repair damaged eye tissue or carry radio and TV signals.

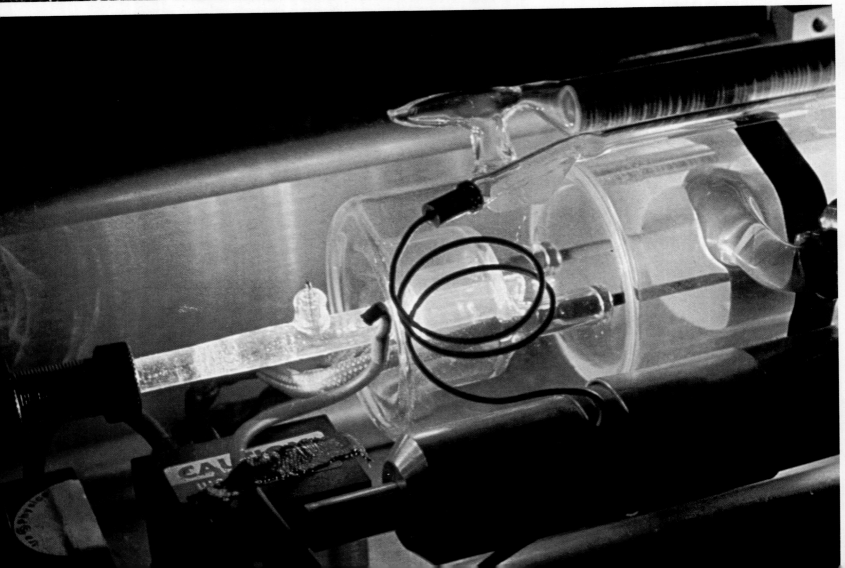

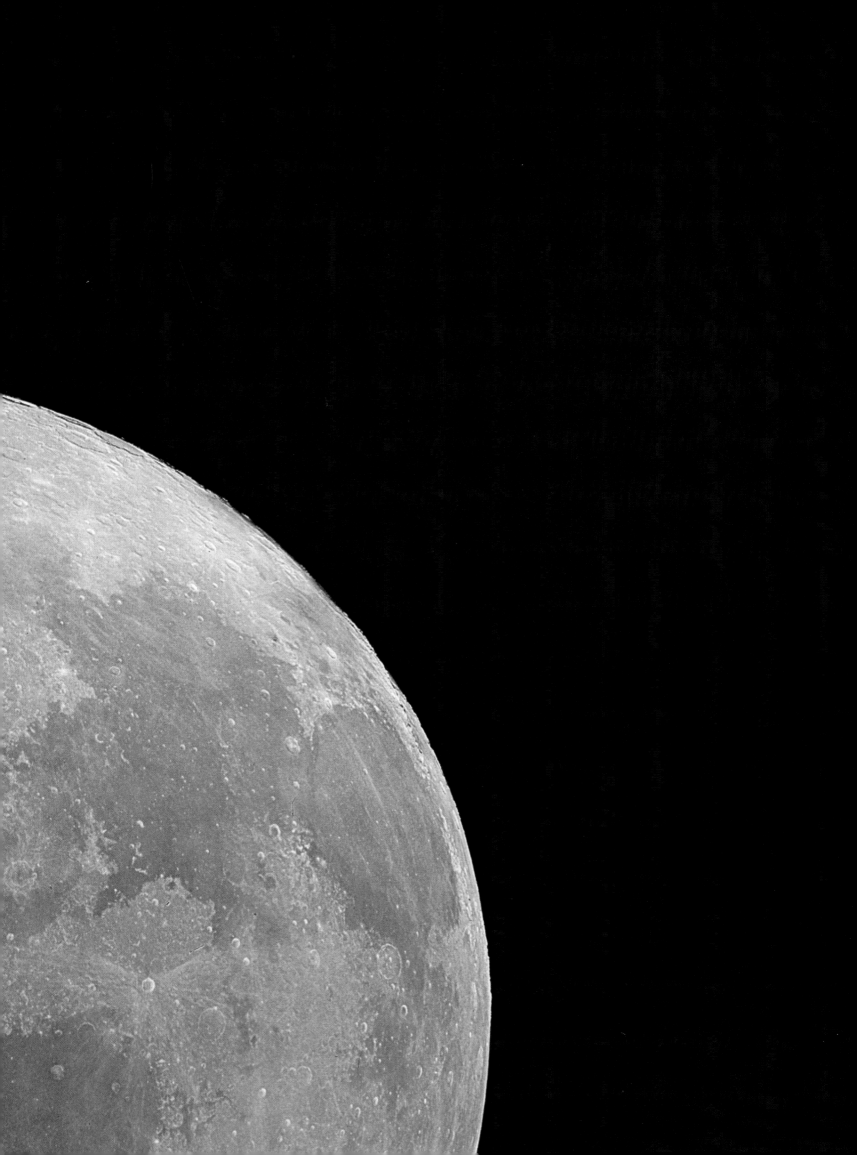

THE EXPLORATION
OF SPACE

The very idea of space exploration is quite amazing to most of us, but we should spare some thought for the means by which it has been accomplished. Space technology has created some of the most wonderful of Man's artefacts – wonders which Antipater of Sidon would have found beyond all belief.

Man has had his eye on the heavens since prehistoric times. Stonehenge, for example, is thought to have been an astronomical aid. It was the invention of the telescope by a Dutch optician, Hans Lippershey, as long ago as 1608, that enabled Galileo and other astronomers to study properly the true nature of the universe. Apart from science fiction writers few people thought seriously about space travel until the 1920s. One of those who did was a Russian schoolmaster, Konstantin Tsiolkovsky. In 1903 he published a paper on the possibility of using rockets for space exploration. Disregarded for many years, his work came to be recognized as the basis for future developments in this field.

Rocket design received a boost during World War II when the German dictator Adolf Hitler wanted a new weapon to use against the Allies. The result was the powerful V2 rocket with which the Germans bombarded Britain in 1944. After the war the Russians and the Americans each took some of the German scientists who had been working on the V2 and made them do further research, both into more sophisticated guided missiles and into space travel. On 4 October 1957, the Russians launched *Sputnik 1*, the world's first man-made satellite. From then on the Russians and Americans launched a succession of space vehicles, some to orbit the Earth, others escaping from the Earth's gravitational field and making their way into outer space. On 12 September 1959 the Russians scored another first with *Luna 2*, which crashlanded on the Moon. The following month *Luna 3* sent back televised pictures of the far side of the Moon which is never visible from Earth. In 1961 Man went into space for the first time when the Russian cosmonaut Yuri Gagarin orbited the Earth aboard the spacecraft *Vostok 1*. It was the beginning of a space race which reached its climax on 20 July 1969, when the American astronauts Neil Armstrong and Edwin Aldrin became the first men to set foot on the Moon. The rocket which boosted them on their journey was the powerful Saturn V. It operated in three stages, the two earlier stages dropping away when the spacecraft was well into its journey.

The complete Moon spacecraft was known as Apollo, and it too was in three parts. The service module contained fuel and other supplies and used rocket motors for steering. It was linked to

the command module in which the astronauts travelled, and to the lunar module, a detachable spacecraft which was able to land on the Moon and take off again. Altogether six Apollo spacecraft landed men on the Moon and brought them safely back. Two members of each Apollo crew actually landed on the Moon while the third piloted the command and service modules in orbit around the Moon. On return to Earth first the lunar module and then the service module were jettisoned, leaving the command module to re-enter Earth's atmosphere and parachute down into the sea.

The actual spacecraft involved in these flights were only the tip of the iceberg in the whole space engineering project. Banks of computers controlled every moment of the flight, radio and television links maintained constant contact between Earth and spacecraft, and every manoeuvre had been rehearsed in simulators designed to reproduce as nearly as possible the conditions of space travel.

The enormous cost of the Moon flights has created different priorities for future space travel. Emphasis is now being placed on the repeated use of space equipment, much of which had to be jettisoned in the early days of space exploration. In the late 1970s, Russians and Americans built orbiting space stations and the American space programme includes a space shuttle vehicle which can take astronauts to space stations and bring them back.

Three other important aspects of space technology are in constant development. Satellites whose orbits have been so precisely calculated that they orbit the Earth at the same speed as the planet's rotation, thus remaining 'stationary' above the surface, are used to monitor the weather and to relay radio and television signals from one part of the world to another. In the sphere of defence, both the United States and the Soviet Union have 'spy' satellites which keep an eye on each other's military activities. The second aspect of space exploration is the use of space probes, unmanned vehicles which travel far out into the solar system, and send back pictures and other data from planets such as Mercury, Venus, Mars, Jupiter, and Saturn. The pictures they transmit are the type of achievements which Antipater of Sidon might once have dreamed of, but which he could never have envisaged as being an everyday occurrence.

Previous pages: **The Earth, with the Moon in the foreground, as seen from the spacecraft *Apollo 10* on its last proving flight before the first lunar landing.**

Right: **A Saturn rocket blasts Apollo 11 off on its historic journey to land two men on the Moon, in July 1969.**

Left: Manned spacecraft and artificial satellites have given a new dimension to the work of geographers and weather forecasters. This space photograph shows a watershed in India, with rivers snaking their way across the the landscape.

Above: Space probes have added enormously to our knowledge of other planets in the Solar System. This comparative 'close-up' of Saturn was taken from a space probe, and shows much more detail than astronomers can see using telescopes on Earth.

Right: The giant radio telescope at Jodrell Bank in Cheshire collects and measures radio waves from space. Jodrell Bank was the first of the giant radio telescopes; there are now many others under construction.

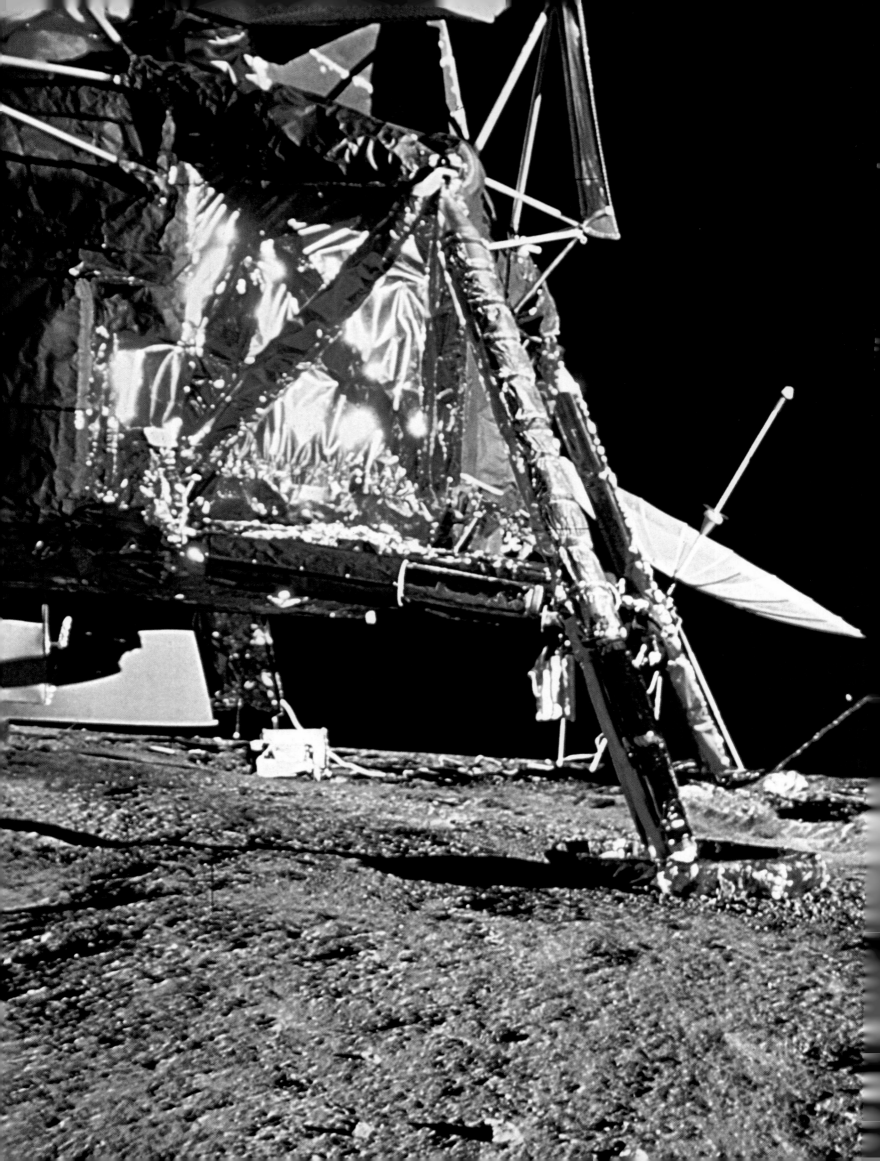

Possibly the greatest man-made wonder of the twentieth century: a lunar landing craft on the moon's surface. This picture is of the second moon landing, by Apollo 12, in November 1969. The astronauts who walked on the moon on this mission were Charles Conrad and Alan Bean, while Richard Gordon circled the Moon in the command module. The astronauts set up a group of six experiments on the Moon to monitor seismic movements, solar radiation, and the Moon's magnetic field. A laser reflector bounced signals back to Earth.

Left: The space-shuttle orbiter *Enterprise* rests on a launching platform. *Enterprise* is the prototype for a new generation of reusable space-craft, and is designed to make up to a hundred orbital missions, being launched by rocket and returning to Earth and landing like a conventional aeroplane. Its long programme of manned test flights began in 1977. The orbiter is designed by American space experts to service a new space laboratory, *Spacelab 1.*

Right: Astronomers have learned a great deal about the three planets nearest to Earth – Mercury, Venus and Mars – from space probes in the American *Mariner* series. This artist's impression shows a Mariner probe nearing Mars. The first probe to orbit Mars was Mariner IX, which photographed the Red Planet from an altitude of 1,970 kilometres (1,225 miles). Other U.S. space probes in the *Viking* series have landed on Mars and sent back data on its soil and atmosphere.

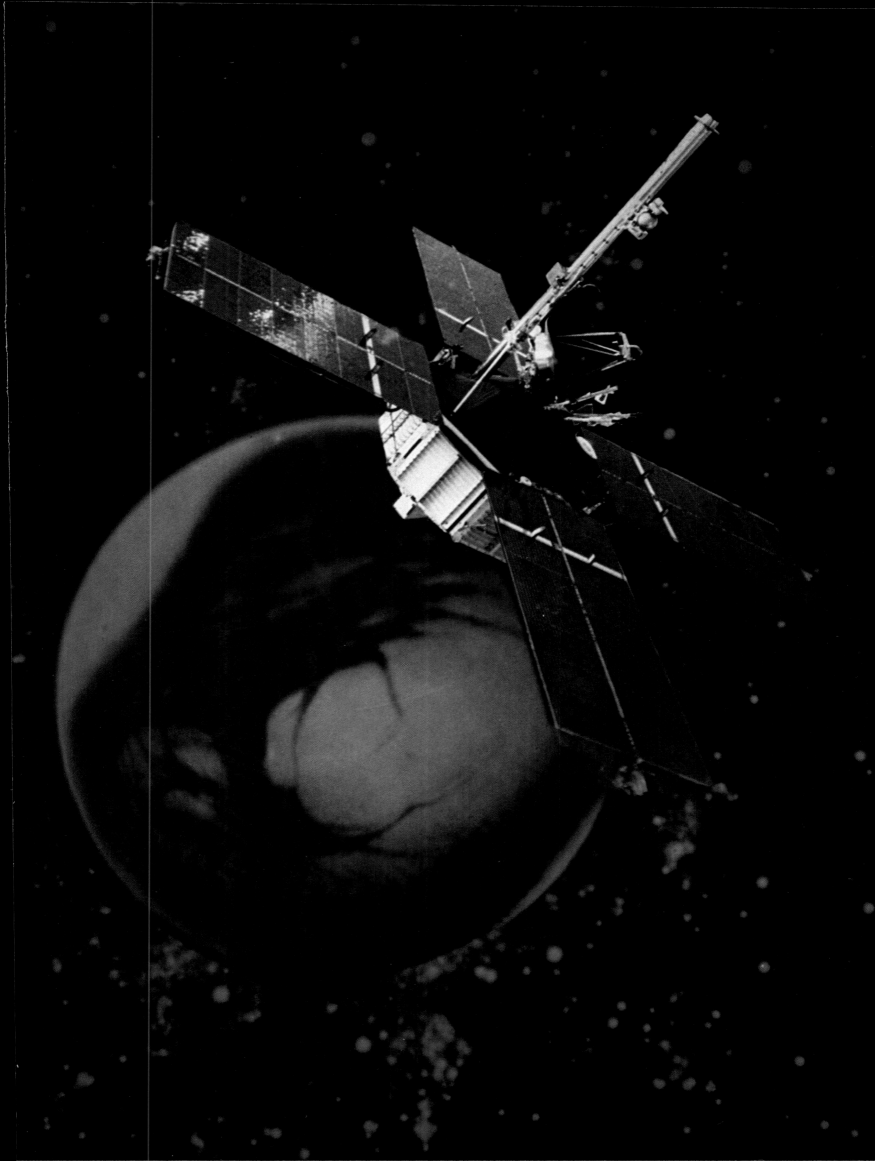

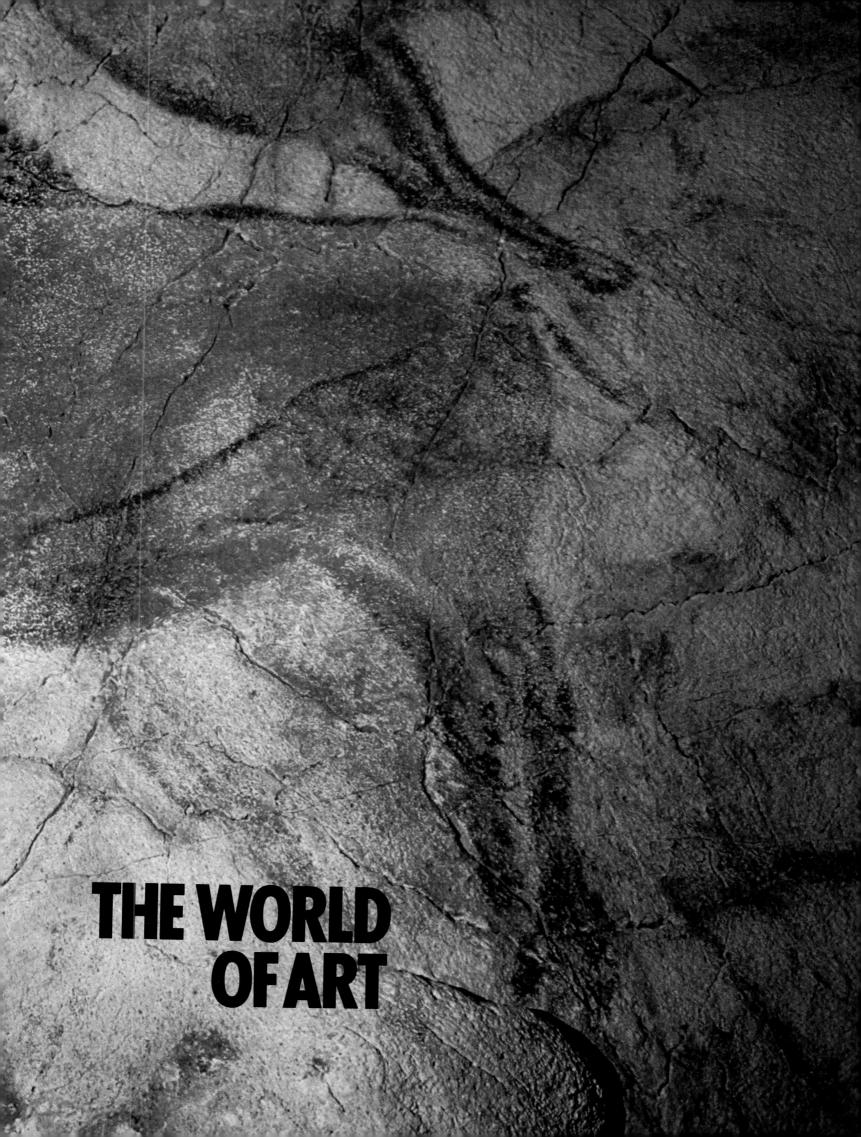

THE WORLD
OF ART

The works of the earliest cave painters are about 30,000 years old. These extraordinary works lay entombed until 1879 when a Spanish antiquary and his daughter, looking round the newly-discovered cave of Altamira in northern Spain, found them. Over one hundred other painted caves have been found since, most in France and Spain. The finest paintings of all are in the cave of Lascaux, near Montignac in France, which were discovered in 1940.

These prehistoric masterpieces have survived for so long because they are on rock and are deep underground, although ironically many less ancient works of art are now lost. However, the works of the Renaissance have survived in abundance and give us a complete record of that marvellous period. Among the most wonderful of the works of the time is the ceiling of the Sistine Chapel in Rome, the product of four years work by Michelangelo Buonarroti between 1508 and 1512. Hardly less remarkable is the fresco of the *Last Judgement*, which he painted in 1534–1541. Two other masterpieces from the Renaissance, *The Last Supper* (ruined almost from the start because the wrong paint was used on a plaster wall) and the enigmatic portrait of *Mona Lisa*, are the works of Leonardo da Vinci.

In sculpture there have been many great works of art, some remarkable for their artistry, some – like the Colossus of Rhodes – for their sheer size. The Statue of Liberty in New York Harbour is the modern counterpart of the Colossus, and is about the same height. It appears taller because it stands on a pedestal. Another sculpture on the grand scale in the United States is the Mount Rushmore National Memorial in the Black Hills of South Dakota. Four huge heads of American presidents are carved into the granite of a cliff, each about 18 metres (60 feet) high.

Colossi were also popular among devotees of Buddhism, and there are many gigantic representations of the Buddha in China, Japan, India and other parts of southern Asia. Among them is the great bronze statue of the Buddha at Kamakura. It stands 15 metres (49 feet) high and is rivalled in size by an image of the Buddha which was carved out of rock at Yün-Kang in China about 700 years earlier.

Size is not by any means the sole criterion that determines greatness in sculpture, and the sculptors of ancient Greece have left a number of much smaller statues of extraordinary beauty. Two examples, unfortunately damaged, deserve a mention. *The Winged Victory of Samothrace*, and the *Venus de Milo*, both still manage to provoke our wonder – they are now in the Louvre Museum in Paris. Outstanding among the many fine statues

of the Renaissance are two by Michelangelo, his *David*, and the version of the *Pieta* which stands in St Peter's, Rome.

Works of art in media other than painting and sculpture must surely include the British Crown Jewels, impressive not only for their artistic merit but for their sheer opulence. The original jewels were broken up in the 1650s after the execution of Charles I but they were remade, incorporating many of the old gems, for the coronation of Charles II in 1660. The oldest jewel is a sapphire which probably belonged to Edward the Confessor, while among the newest is the Star of Africa, the world's largest cut diamond, and part of the Cullinan diamond which was found in South Africa in 1905.

As a collection, the treasure taken from the tomb of the boy-pharaoh Tutankhamun is without doubt one of the greatest artistic wonders, and astonishing not only for its beauty but also for the fact that it survived when the tombs of every other pharaoh were plundered. The gem of the collection is the gold mask which was found covering the face of the pharaoh.

Finally, there is a collection of a very different kind: the stained glass windows of Chartres Cathedral in France. Stained glass is often very beautiful in itself, but the windows of Chartres, dating from the 13th century, with their profusion of glass which glows and sparkles as the light streams through them, are so beautiful and awesome that there is little difficulty in putting them among the finest works of art.

It is really quite impossible to represent photographically the individual's experience of literature and music. However, that is no reason why they should not be mentioned, for they figure considerably among the greatest works of art. The works of Shakespeare, Marvell, Milton, Pope, George Eliot, Henry James and T.S. Eliot, for example, are in their own way great, as are the works of Vivaldi, Mozart, Beethoven and Schubert.

They are concerned not with improving our environment or the practical workings of our daily lives, but with a way of understanding, both intellectually and emotionally, the quality of life.

Nonetheless, the wealth of experience communicated through such works, combined with the achievements of the visual arts, establish a body of works which are undoubtedly as great as, if not greater than, the finest works of science.

Previous pages: The 'Standing Bison' in the cave at Altamira, in Spain, was painted about 30,000 years ago.

Right: The solid gold mask found in the tomb of Pharaoh Tutankhamun. It is inlaid with lapis lazuli, strips of blue glass, and precious stones.

Above: This Japanese print, although made about 1900, typifies the simple style of traditional Japanese art. Prints of this kind are known as *ukiyo-ye.* Many depicted scenes from plays and they were produced in large numbers from the mid-1700s onwards. This print records a unique Japanese art form, the tea ceremony, which is many centuries old.

Left: In the days before printing it was the custom to illuminate valuable and important books with miniature paintings and other designs. This page comes from the *Book of Hours* (a prayer book for laymen) made for Jeanne of Savoy. The artist was Jehan Pucelle, a French illuminator, who worked in Paris during the first half of the 14th century.

Far left: The 'Golden Victim of Bangkok', one of many gigantic statues of the Buddha which are to be found all over southern and eastern Asia. This gilded statue is suffering badly from two aspects of modern civilization: pollution, which is affecting its finish, and traffic vibration, which has produced a number of cracks. Statues of the Buddha are aids to contemplation, and not objects of worship.

Far left: A Renaissance masterpiece – *The Virgin of the Rocks*, by Leonardo da Vinci. It is one of comparatively few paintings which he completed. Leonardo painted two versions of this picture: this one is in the National Gallery in London; the other is in Paris.

Above: The Bathers (detail), by Georges Seurat, is a product of the French Impressionist movement which revolutionized the world of art in the 1800s. The picture was first exhibited in 1884. Seurat developed a style of painting known as pointillism, using dots of colour rather than strokes of the brush.

Left: A detail from Impressions of Africa, 1938, a painting by the Spanish Surrealist artist Salvador Dali. Dali and his fellow Surrealists produced pictures in which they tried to show the imaginings of the subconscious.

Left: The Venus de Milo is one of the finest surviving examples of ancient Greek sculpture. It was found in an underground room on the island of Melos in 1820, having been hidden for centuries. Missing pieces of the arms which were found with it later disappeared. The statue was probably carved in the 2nd century BC, and was based on a Corinthian statue carved some 200 years earlier.

Right: Perhaps one of the greatest paintings of the Renaissance is the *Last Judgement*, which Michelangelo painted on the wall of the Sistine Chapel in the Vatican. He painted it between the years 1534 and 1541, having earlier spent four years painting his most famous work, the ceiling of the chapel. Here, the painting forms a background to Pope Paul VI as he addresses a synod of bishops.

The glowing colours of the
stained-glass windows in
Chartres Cathedral, seen
with the sunshine behind
them, are high among the
man-made wonders of the
world. Most of the glass was
made between 1215 and
1240 by French craftsmen,
and the majority of the
windows were gifts from the
guilds – goldsmiths, masons,
carpenters, builders, bakers
and others – the trade union
movement of the day. The
Charlemagne window, *left*,
was donated by the furriers'
guild. The North Rose, *right*,
was the gift of the French
Royal Family. It shows kings
of Israel, and St Anne. The
centre of the five lancet
windows below it is dedicated
to St Anne. This saint was
held in high regard at
Chartres. Her skull had been
looted by Crusaders from
Constantinople, and was
donated to the cathedral in
1205.

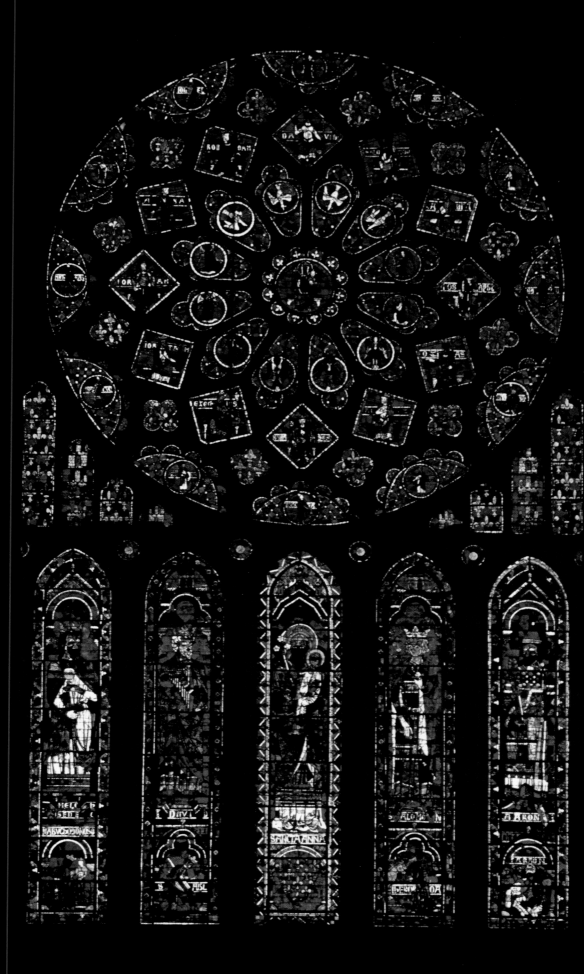

Not all man-made wonders are artefacts, things you can see and touch. Many of the greatest works of art are in a medium that calls for them to be recreated every time they are seen or heard. Here, the excitement of music and dance are shown as Margot Fonteyn and Rudolf Nureyev dance the title rôles in Serge Prokofiev's ballet *Romeo and Juliet*, with members of London's Royal Ballet Company.

INDEX

References in italics are to illustrations

Acknowledgements

The publishers would like to thank the following individuals and organizations for their kind permission to reproduce the photographs in this book:

Heather Angel/Biofotos 16; Aspect 77 above; Bio-Arts (David Burn) 40 inset; Boymans van Beuningen Museum, Rotterdam/A.D.A.G.P., Paris (1980) (Painting by Salvador Dali) 89 below; Colorific (A. Gibson) 46–47; Richard Cooke 49; The Cooper-Bridgeman Library 66; The Daily Telegraph Colour Library (Tony Marshall) 67 below, (J.G. Mason) 80; Bob Davis/Aspect 31 right; Zoe Dominic 94–95; Robert Estall 30–31, 77 below; An Esso Photograph 44 below; Sonia Halliday Photographs 8–9, 53, 92, 93; Robert Harding Picture Library 85; The John Hillelson Agency Ltd. (Ted Spiegel) 91; Michael Holford Photographs Title Page, (Bob Estall) 17, 50–51, 63, 64 below, 65, 67 above, 82–83, 87 above and below, 90; Angelo Hornak 22 above; By Courtesy of The Italian State Tourist Office (E.N.I.T.) 34; L. Alex Langley/Aspect 23; LAT Photographic 43; The Henry Moore Foundation Contents; NASA/Colorific 75; Reproduced by Courtesy of The Trustees, The National Gallery, London 88, 89 above; Octopus Books Ltd. 42 above, (Nicky Wright) 42 below, (Bergstrom and Boyle) 70 below; Oxford Scientific Films Ltd. 70 above; Photri 81; Picturepoint – London Endpapers, 14, 18–19, 22 below, 28 inset, 55 below, 59 above and below, 76, 78–79; Popperfoto (Ambrose Greenway) 45, 72–73; Science Museum, London/Crown Copyright 40–41; Spectrum Colour Library 7, 11, 15 above, 35, 55 above, 64 above; John W.R. Taylor 47 inset right, 48 below; Transworld Feature Syndicate (UK) Ltd. (Andy Levin) 21, (Fred Ward) 27 above, 56–57, (Alan Orling) 57 right, (John Launois) 86; United Kingdom Atomic Energy Authority Photographic Library 71; Vision International (Angelo Hornak) 20, (Paolo Koch) 28–29, (Angelo Hornak) 58, (Steve Herr) 60–61; John Watney 68 inset left and right, 68–69; Zefa Picture Library (UK) Ltd. (L. Hrdlicka) Half Title, (K. Kerth) 12–13, (G. Ricatto) 15 below, (D. Baglin) 24–25, (J. Schörken) 32, (K. Kerth) 33, (Orion Warashina) 36–37, (J.M. Jarvis) 39, (Foto Leidmann) 44 above, (W.L. Hamilton) 47 inset left, (Konrad Helbig) 48 above, (R. Everts) 54.